Quiéreme

Juliana Delgado Lopera

NOMADIC PRESS

OAKLAND

111 FAIRMOUNT AVENUE
OAKLAND, CA 94611

BROOKLYN

475 KENT AVENUE #302
BROOKLYN, NY 11249

WWW.NOMADICPRESS.ORG

MASTHEAD

FOUNDING AND MANAGING EDITOR
J. K. FOWLER

ASSOCIATE EDITOR
MICHAELA MULLIN

DESIGN
J. K. FOWLER

MISSION STATEMENT

Nomadic Press is a 501 (C)(3) not-for-profit organization that supports the works of emerging and established writers and artists. Through publications (including translations) and performances, Nomadic Press aims to build community among artists and across disciplines.

SUBMISSIONS

Nomadic Press wholeheartedly accepts unsolicited book manuscripts. To submit your work, please visit www.nomadicpress.org/submissions

DISTRIBUTION

Orders by trade bookstores and wholesalers:
Small Press Distribution,
1341 Seventh Street
Berkeley, CA 94701
spd@spdbooks.org
(510) 524-1668 / (800) 869-7553

Quiéreme

This book was made possible by a loving community of chosen family and friends, old and new.

For author questions or to book a reading at your bookstore, university/school, or alternative establishment, please send an email to info@nomadicpress.org.

Cover and back artwork by Arthur Johnstone

Published by Nomadic Press, 111 Fairmount Avenue, Oakland, CA 94611

Third printing, 2019

Printed in the United States of America

LIBRARY OF CONGRESS CATALOGING-IN-PUBLICATION DATA

Delgado Lopera, Juliana, 1988 –
Title: *Quiéreme*
P. CM.
Summary: There's really no literal translation of "Quiéreme"; it's in between "like me" and "love me" but, unlike in English, the verb does all the work: a command packed with feeling; a want; a little ball full of longing. And that's basically what this book is: a little thing full of longing (and essays). In Spanglish. From loving imaginary people in Catholic school, to waiting for a lover's tears at the airport, to documenting post-breakup grief, "Quiéreme" is a call on all the lingering ghosts of loving.

[1. LOVE. 2. QUEER STUDIES. 3. AMERICAN GENERAL.] I. III. TITLE.

2017937391
ISBN: 978-0-9981348-4-0

Quiéreme

Juliana Delgado Lopera

NOMADIC
PRESS

para Laura

CONTENTS

13 THE BOY WHO NEVER CRIED FOR ME

19 THE FAKE PEOPLE I'VE LOVED

25 GENTRIFY MY HEART

31 QUIÉREME

"You wait for me where I do not want to go: you love me where I do not exist."

– Roland Barthes, *A Lover's Discourse*

"We went our separate ways, but within walking distance of one another."

– Patti Smith, *Just Kids*

THE BOY WHO NEVER CRIED FOR ME

In this story, Miami is the Promised Land. The Promised Land steaming with floating particles of piss, tanning lotion, my mama's Revlon dark rouge lipstick mixed with my tía's spit propelled out of her mouth as she dragged our bags out into the airport parking lot, as she chewed bubblegum while yelling, *THIS IS MIAMI, DON'T YOU SEE? WE GOT A WHITE VAN, mira mira. See the white van? See it? HERE IN MIAMI WE GOT A VAN AND AIR CONDITIONING. DID YOU BRING THE BREAD? Mueche a ver, dónde está el pan? HOW WAS THE PLANE RIDE? LIKE SHIT I SUPPOSE. EVERYTHING IN COLOMBIA IS MIERDA MIERDA MIERDA.* And, *WHY ARE YOU CRYING? WHY IS SHE CRYING? You see that? That's our white van!*

After the three-hour plane ride they greeted us with a prayer and we greeted them with smashed bread bought at eight in the morning that day at a local panadería millions of kilometers away. *This bread smells like Colombia,* my tía said, as she bit on the pancito con uvas pasas, and I could not tell if it was a good or a bad thing. Twelve years later, when I ask my sister what's the first thing she remembers of our arrival to Miami, she says the smell: *it smelled like white people.* Then she corrects herself: *I thought it was the way gringos smelled, but I realize now that it was just the air-conditioning and these make-believe hollow walls.*

Did you cry? I ask her. *Do you remember crying?*

Duh, Juliana, why you asking stupid questions again? she says, handing my mama the phone.

Here's the deal: That day, we'd left Bogotá PARA SIEMPRE, and I remember asking my boyfriend to finger me one last time in the airport bathroom. I stroked his beard, played with his greasy hair, asked him if he would visit me in Miami. Was he sad I was leaving? But was he *real* sad?

Pablo, I said, *we're never seeing each other again. Never. Do you understand what that means?*

He gave me his dirty Casio watch, a baby-blue digital thing that beeped every hour and was way too big for my wrists. Biting on his pierced lip, he mumbled some communist shit about love—of course, that's what Pablo would do—quote some Zapatista motherfucker while I was trying to get him to cry. Give me a history lesson about the Mexican revolution while I internally bit my lip, my tongue, my bored-as-fuck heart, wanting him to touch me, wanting him to cry, wanting him to break into song like René from Salserín (girl, don't judge) and drown every policía bachiller in this verraco airport with his tears.

Ever since Mami informed us we were moving to Mee-a-mee with our tías, I couldn't wait for that moment of sobbing at the airport, that moment when my boy's heart would rip, bounce into the tile floor, land in my hands so I could care for it like a dying bunny. All my girlfriends were there: fifteen Catholic school uniforms munching on Happy Meals. I knew this was my last moment to shine, that after lying about every single Camilo, Diego, Daniel, Roberto, after writing myself love letters in ugly boy handwriting, after tricking my sister into sucking on my neck, and after sucking on mangos and pineapples for hours to convince everyone I was the mera mera queen of dick or whatever, leaving the country *forever* was the perfect drama-infused opportunity for a boy to declare his love to me. And this was a real bone-flesh boyfriend—your average trigueñito colombiano, but still—I had broken up with all the imaginary ones.

Everyone had to see this: that I could be loved, that someone could love me like this, that this eighteen-year-old criollito kid was about to lose his shit over this fifteen-year-old long-gone pussy.

I wanted to squeeze every bit of dramatic tension I could out of the four hours spent at El Dorado Airport. I wanted my Daniela Romo moment. I was Daniela Romo, carajo, *me.* Because qué carajo this migration and the Avianca plane. Qué carajo our lives packed in two Samsonite bags, the merengue I wouldn't hear again for two years flowing from the nearby cafeteria. *Wilfrido, mi amor, you're only missed in exile.* Qué carajo Mami's blow-dried hair hiding our collective sadness and my sister's clueless glossy eyes and my other tía chain-smoking and some guy I've never seen hugging Mami, kissing her neck. Qué carajo the pieces of ourselves that refused to leave. The pieces that never left and are still roaming at El Dorado, forever stuck drinking watered-down tintos. Qué carajo, cachaco, qué clase de misunderstanding. And the cleaning lady in the bathroom throwing a puta side-eye, the Fabuloso smell, the roscón I barely ate because of nausea, the cordillera boycotting my ass for leaving mi patria, the Bon Bon Bums sticking out of my bag, the knots on my arms, my ribcage. Qué carajo irse. MAMITA, THIS WAS MY DANIELA ROMO MOMENT. I only wanted his tears.

When we eat our Happy Meals, all the girls cry. All the girls but me. My fifteen girlfriends plus my sister's fifteen girlfriends, all sobbing, snorting snot, asking for napkins, then sobbing again, snorting snot, asking for napkins, then sobbing again, snorting snot, asking for napkins. You get the picture. But yours truly? Na-nais, not one drop of water. Some girls cried so intensely, their entire faces covered by a thin transparent film of snot, like they'd been eating pussy for five hours and now it dripped, mixed with the Happy Meal cheese, all going back inside their mouths where it started.

Juli, they say, *Juli, marica, huevón, Juli, qué mierda marica, qué mierda.* None of them finish their sentences.

We're at the McDonalds on the corner of the second floor, you know, of the old airport with the pink floors and low ceilings and una musiquita in the background, interrupted every five minutes with an update on Fulanita's stolen purse, Sutanita missing the plane, María X-Y-Z please pick up your child at the Avianca counter. Every so often, this omnipresent voice reminding us we're gone, we're not even here anymore, please, international passengers, proceed to migración—the plane already left with us in it. Mi reina, we're already mas allá que acá. But I refuse to hear the intercom or Mami's exasperated hands gesturing to me to behave or my sister's cry for another Sharpie so Margarita can finish writing a friendship love letter on her school shirt.

I stare at Pablo, trying to figure out what his crying game is. He's focused on licking an Oreo McFlurry and handing out napkins to all the lloronas. My friends all think he's such a papasito, how lucky I am to have him, look at that beard and those brown eyes, and, mi reina, he *knows* how to dress. But the papasito doesn't shed a tear. The papasito and I have been dating for two months, which in teenager years is a *lifetime* full of passionate love, mixtapes, unfulfilled promises, and, in Pablo's case, too many ideological rants. He smiles at me, grabs my hand, draws circles inside my palm, kisses my neck. He writes TE AMO with his index finger on my jeans in all caps. He swears he'll visit, swears we'll get married in freaking Villa De Leyva papá (to the grand amusement of my mother who, years later, chuckled, calling us unos pobres culicagados), swears with whispers and slimy kisses that I don't return because I'm fucking furious, because there's only twenty minutes left before we have to line up for customs and Pablo, mi amor, dónde están tus tears? I want to take them with me.

Years later, when I ask Mami about that day at the airport, she says she remembers the mayonnaise taste of the Big Mac and the ugly green sweater your boyfriend gave you, nena, and your tía Dominique who wasn't there. She didn't make it to the airport. She had to be hospitalized that morning because of heartbreak. Se le rompió el corazón, it was all too much for her. And your amigas, por Dios, crying como si se estuviera acabando el mundo.

But the world was *ending, Ma, no?*

Masomenos.

Pero, like, did you *cry, Ma?*

It takes her a moment to answer. I can hear my sister yelling in the background, the fridge in my mom's house opening and closing, Christian music making its way to the phone.

I didn't cry, she says proudly. *I was keeping it together for you.*

I know it's time to go into customs because Mami's face changes to a nervous smile as she gathers her purse, her coat, the passports, one last bite into that Colombian Big Mac. Her jet black hair one wave of sadness. She doesn't say anything, but she doesn't have to. The waves of her perfect straightened hair pull us into action—hair straightened that same morning in a house that is not our house by a window with no view, straightened flawless at six in the morning while Mami thought nobody but the hairdresser saw her scribbling invisible notes to my father. Invisible notes to herself. While she bid adiós to the damn city, the damn life en este país de mierda from a window with no view. Este país de mierda that we will never miss because, cachaco, nos vamos pa'l norte, a la Promised Land. Y este país de mierda that we will never leave, that we're leaving right now as we kiss good-bye the rows of onlookers that are our life, este país de mierda will be nothing but a shadow, nothing but a ghost que baila pegadito.

The waves of her hair call on us. And I'm almost done with my ice cream, but still no tears from Pablo. I'm passive-aggressively scooping ice cream, jamming it in my mouth, vanilla dripping from the corners of my lips onto the floor. The last time Mami ate ice cream, she was divorcing my father over some cookies and cream with arequipe. She didn't cry then either. Not in front of us. Mami had this thing where she locked herself in the bathroom for hours with a notebook, a pen, and a yellow highlighter. She then came out with a new family plan, all energized like nothing had happened, ignoring the sadness that had fueled her, yellow stains covering her mouth and palms. I braided her hair after. I combed and braided it while she went on and on about the new life plans she had for us girls, us three girls. She took notes about our life, she had a plan. This was the plan. La Promised Land and the white van. The ice cream dripping from my mouth was part of it.

My fucking boyfriend now only chuckling, of course, and I'm toda emputada, toda heated up, toda que te mato, Pablo, for killing my dreams, because you're supposed to be just water right now, just a well of sadness begging and pulling me to you, you're supposed to give me five reasons to stay, you're supposed to rip that passport in two, supposed to heal Mami's heart with Vick Vaporú, clean her mouth and palms so she never joins my tías and their white van, you're supposed to lick the ice cream as it drips and bring it back to me.

Pero, mi reina, we never really leave.

We cross the charco with a bag full of feelings, a somber look, and jars of Vick Vaporú to heal Mami's heart. We never leave. We don't really know how to. We climb into that plane like a herd of sheep after swearing to the customs guy this is a trip to Disney World, señor, ain't nobody gonna stay in some muggy-ass swamp full of rednecks and crocodiles. Mami had my sister and I practice saying, *Hola, señor de la aduana, we're going to Disney World.* Again, she'd say to us in front of the bathroom mirror. *Hola, señor de la aduana*, we'd say in unison, *we're going to Disney World. No, señor, we don't plan on overstaying, we have a life back home, we have a house back home, I have a boyfriend back home who cries for me.*

When we eat the smashed bread with my tías after landing in Miami, my grandmother is there, too. It's like when we were all in Bogotá, but instead of wearing black and gray, instead of having antique, gothic, creepy porcelain dolls as ornaments around the house, they're all wearing fucking pastels, Bermudas, flip-flops. They are all sweating. Nobody can smoke inside the house, and they're all proud to have 'made it.' La Promised

Land, cachaco, te cuento. They're giving us a rundown of how shit happens around here. *We're in Miami now,* they say, *esto es Estados Unidos.*

Pero, like, we're still in Bogotá. Todavía because, te digo, we never really leave. Because I don't understand what leaving means. I don't know it takes months, years, decades to leave. That I'll always be stuck at that airport. That we would fly on a plane, land in a swamp, grow mold on our eyes from the humidity, scales on our chests from the air-conditioning. That even when we landed, even when the Florida sun outside dared us to die fried, lonely, and wearing three-dollar Walmart leggings, even when the TV promised INGLES SIN BARRERAS, the barrera was already there, the barrera never moves, never softens.

When we're on the plane, my sister cries. Mami holds our hands in prayer, and I look out at the cordillera and think about Pablo's dry motherfucking eyes as mine water. All I can do is imagine Daniela Romo. I call the goddess to sit with me and hold me, wrap me in that thick, gorgeous mane of hers, and rock me until I'm a plátano maduro, until I ripen into something more, something beautiful.

THE FAKE PEOPLE I'VE LOVED

"I dreamed that you bewitched me into bed
And sung me moon-struck, kissed me quite insane.
(I think I made you up inside my head.)"

- Sylvia Plath, "Mad Girl's Love Song"

The story went like this: Camilo waited for me at the park next to my house every day after school. He brought Bon Bon Bum (look it up), cigarettes, and his tongue inside my mouth. He said, *Quibo, qué mas? I like you.* After he left, I walked two blocks north to another park where Pablo under a hoodie munched Sparkies, also smoked cigarettes (although red Marlboros, so ew), and wrote me—ME who was barely twelve—a love poem. It was heaven-like. I was twelve and totally killing it. My friends envied me! Should I tell you about Darío, my *third* boyfriend? Darío in a leatherjacket while I stroked his greasy brown hair, a leftist revolutionary wearing Zapatista shirts, a beard, etc. . . . I had not one, not two, but un-dos-TRES boyfriends (I know, and there you sat thinking I was *just* an angry lesbian).

The next day, I arrived early and giddy from so much excitement at my all-girl Catholic school. Really-quick: picture nuns, picture impeccable uniform, picture Jesús bleeding from the cross everywhere you look, picture this humble narrator in a ponytail and yellow headband (the 90s mi reina). Inside the classroom I whispered to all my girlfriends about my romantic whereabouts the night before. *His tongue! His mouth! His index finger! His poetry!* I showed them the poem, a letter, and the plastic wrap of the Bon Bon Bum as proof of my escapades. Sometimes this was enough, and by the end of first period most of them believed my triumphant romances. Other times, some girls' skepticism made me repeat *Uva Curuba Uva* until my upper lip folded into two perfect semicircles proving I was not a mouth virgin, proving I was kissed the night before.

Sidenote: Uva Curuba Uva *was a game some girls played in their prepubescent years asking each other to say said phrase over and over. If your upper lip folded into two perfect semicircles at the center you were not a mouth virgin, someone had kissed you. You earned a new status, etc. I know, go figure.*

The truth is: I've been having relationships with fake people since the beginning of my time in this precious mama earth (let's be honest you probably have, too, and we could all start a support group together). The truth is: I was enthralled by the attention my storytelling received among the chicas. Every day after school I sat on my desk jotting down a different plotline for each of my boyfriends. I had a notebook separated with each name (color-coded) so I wouldn't get them confused. They were *fleshed-out* characters I tell you. I knew their smells (cold medicine, Doritos, cheap cologne), I knew their fears (spiders, tampons, curling irons), I knew what they wanted (a new car, a hot shower, a small revolution in my pants), I understood their complicated relationships with their mothers and why their fathers wanted to enroll them in military school. It was, all in all, amor del bueno que no se lo lleva el viento.

I wanted to grow up so quickly!

Wait, no, scratch that.

It was not about growing up but about pushing the limits of my imagination and the boundaries of believability among my peers which, as you can see, were pretty stretchy (I mean, we believed Papi Dios spoke through the tiny speck of white beard attached to our elderly priest).

Anyway, mi vida, some may suggest this was the beginning of my unstoppable lesbianism and in retrospect, I realized I was compensating for the gay monster wakening inside me that eventually took over and said: Na-*ha* mami, we like them girls. But in that moment I had so much time on my hands! I was so fascinated with the possibility of love and tongue-kissing and Colombian telenovelas (there she goes essentializing her people! Well, *duh*). Catholic school both ruined and pushed my imagination in fucked-up and feminist ways. It was expected that I imagined and believed this holy supernatural world where seas parted and people turned to salt. In very heterosexist ways reality inside Catholicism was rarely palpable: reality was twelve men in robes munching bread alongside The Messiah (talk about homos), and my womanhood had its genesis in some guy's ribs.

A ver, do you see the pattern here? My three boyfriends were just my own extension of Bible stories, and then some.

To all this add a weekly mass paired with militant telenovela watching because, déjame decirte, there is no one more dramatic than Mary Magdalene and Jesús in the same room as Gaviota from *Café, Con Aroma de Mujer* or Juana Valentina from *Las Juanas*—two telenovelas I watched religiously. I wanted passion, I wanted to be desired, and I wanted someone to die for me—and if possible, to be whipped and crucified (which has yet to happen). I wasn't seeking out these boys in real life because that would have been too boring (and none were willing to play crucifixion). When you are a prepúber, real-life boys are to yawn for. I wanted the desire to be crafted my way, even if that desire was born out of hello the most patriarchal system ever (how you doing queridísimo Pope!), I had agency to create, sculpt, and intensify that desire as I pleased: I owned the remote control of *their* imaginary longing.

Yes, at twelve I had my own set of feminist Colombian boys which, believe me, is rare. Three handsome boys who—like Jesús Abraham and María—lived in a drawer of my imagination.

The three boys were not the first or the last fake people I loved (but they're memorable and I keep them close to my heart). Leni was my imaginary friend up until my eleventh birthday. I cherished this relationship deeply. We were BFFs. I still have memories of seven-year-old me peeing while Leni stood next to the shower chatting it up about how my mom's new haircut was una nota! I dressed in my father's running shorts, used my mother's pearls, and smeared makeup all over my face. He did the same. It was Role Playing 101. I drew a picture of Leni that was lost in The Big Migration, osea when I moved from Bogotá to Florida eleven years ago. But you can always call my mamá and she'll verify Leni's existence. My mother is (always) more than happy to talk to you about my imaginary friends and to give you a detailed account of the fictive people taking over my life.

On the subject of fictive people: you may be thinking, she's probably over this now that she's an adult (barely, really, and struggling), right? Sure, we all had our batch of imaginary girlfriends / boyfriends in our childhood, but that's what children do. But at twenty-six, you should be purged of fantasizing about the non-existent. At twenty-six, those are pendejadas! Mariconerías! Cosas de culicagada! Signs of some truly unresolved daddy and mommy issues (also another story).

Well, mi reina, I'm a fiction writer, my official title is Person Who Makes Up Other People and Makes Them Breathe. How can this be accomplished without falling for some of them? How can I not fall say, for instance, for (fictive) Michele Bachmann when in this story I wrote she's clearly in pain—still homophobic and Republican—but somehow capable of love and intimacy with a certain María. Michele shows her tulip tattoo! And María braids Michele's hair! And they hold hands in the dark! (*Mrs. Bachmann, if you're reading this, I wrote a story about you and I think you should give lesbianism a chance. Just think about it*).

Some writers are able to keep distance from their "fictional people," but, let's be honest, I don't. The truth is I never stopped having these relationships, no mi amor, not even close:

1. When I first moved to Miami I pretended my math teacher was my lover and we walked around Floridian lakes holding hands. She also wrote me letters that I wrote every day during my job at Payless.
2. The Christian dancer in the story I submitted for graduate school still haunts me in my dreams (or while awake).
3. I've stopped people on the street thinking they are one of my three feminist boys.
4. For one year, I pretended that Sylvia Plath lived inside of me and wanted to use my body to carroy out the remaining years of her writing career.

You *see*?

There is nothing more feminist than being able to imagine and long for possible worlds outside our own. To be able to create worlds that push the boundaries of normal, that house the deviant, that redefine hierarchies; to imagine is to resist. Imagining is a verb, an action. This is what I do daily. This is what Catholic school taught me (among other things). This is what Darío, Pablo, Leni, Michele, Sylvia, are for me: an opening of possibility. I cannot conceive of a life without this longing (and I don't want to).

And then, on one gloomy Bogotá morning, my fake boyfriend and I were invited to So and So's party. My girlfriends were eager to finally meet my boyfriend, and they wouldn't take no for an answer. I did what any teenager in a dangerous city would do in the 90s: I went online (dial-up) to a chat room, I got me a boyfriend named Darío Gómez (sí, my fellow Colombians, like the fucking singer), and asked him to meet me outside So and So's house. *Yes, yes, I realize how lucky I was that the kid was not a psycho old man (a guardian Angel by the last name of Plath looking over me)*. The point is, when he arrived, I debriefed him on everything he had to say and the kid was down for it! (Darío wherever you are, thank you, homie.) Everyone believed the story. I went to that party with my real fake boyfriend Darío Gómez and made out the entire night.

GENTRIFY MY HEART

When the Pastora says, *Cómo están los hijos de Dios?*, you say, *Estamos vivos en Jesucristo*. When the Pastora shuts her eyes, you extend your arms to her in prayer and secretly hope she picks you to share your life testimony today, only this time you promise God not to stutter, not to pee your pants a little. You watch your mama's hands in virgin-praying mode as the salsa beats from the alabanza drown the murmur of the ujieres in the back still trying to usher in people who keep kissing, shaking hands, blessing each other. *Hermana! Hermano! Batiendo palma a lo que da.* The mamis eye each other, scanning each other's holiness up and down, searching for any remnants of the devil on each other's tight pink dresses, their straightened hair, the way their kids color the Espíritu Santo.

The men are, well, men. Silky shirts, chest hair, enough patchouli to kill a continente. Before the excited Pastor takes the stage, your mama points with determination to the men and whispers, *Soon, nena, you will find a good Christian man.* And there are so many Christian men, but when you look at them with those droopy bored immigrant eyes, you don't see wedding, you don't see bebés, you see brown thick thighs blurring your view, and instead of holding that dude's hand, you're diving deep into her pussy. Your mama holds your hand. *A good man, mi amor. Amén.*

At church, we learn Dios es grande. Dios es amor. Dios es vida. Homeboy is so big not even your biggest tío can cross him, nor your rehabilitated cousin leading the youth group, nor your energized grandma shaking it with the cane. If something is off in your life, hermana, it is because you haven't prayed enough. It's a result of your wrongdoing.

Don't think you understand what I'm saying, queen, because you don't.

Dios is not here for the wishy-washy, the lukewarm, the motherfuckers just calentando silla who, once out of His house, forget to follow His footsteps (footsteps packaged in a two-hour lecture by the Pastor for your convenience, hermano). Dios is not here for the man with man, the woman with woman, the weird hijos de su madre sashaying ese culo close to satanás. Not here for the cultural Catholics either, thinking that just because their Vatican papis wear Prada, they hold Diosito's greater truth. Na-ha, cachaco. Truth swims in sound bites and cumbia beats inside a rented room in the Hyatt hotel somewhere in north Miami. It is preached by two tacky Barranquilleros with two kids and no sense of humor. Two hermanos evangelizing in the name of Jesucristo so that all Colombians in Miami may purge themselves from sin. Especially the homo sin.

As the Pastores explain, Papi Dios is up there watching you smoke that cigarette, watching that finger swimming close to your tesorito, watching you build a life in His palabra so when the apocalypse arrives, you, mi hermano, don't burn in hell. All children of God will be lifted to His glory if—and only if—they follow His Word closely.

And Papi Dios knows.

He knows when you buy unholy cereal, knows when you're undressing the new girl from the youth group con esa mirada or even *think* of dancing reggaetón. He knows when you lock yourself in the church bathroom doing perico lines off your Bible, thinking up ways to Greyhound away, but to where? In Miami, you're too lazy, mi reina, to think this plan through. Instead, you wash your hands and peak at that girl's perky teticas before squirming away and sitting next to Mami again. And God knows. He knows how you feel, and He's here to change that. But first, you gotta let him into your heart. Because for Dios, for *this* God, life is black and white. You're either on his winning holy team or your losing big-time, you drunk sodomizer son-of-a-bitch. For this God, His Colombian Christian children are up here, while the rest of satanic humanity is choosing to swim with the worms.

My mama knows all of this, but I don't.

She fell head over heels in love with the Piedra Angular church when we moved from Bogotá to Miami, when I was fifteen. It wasn't Mami's idea to suddenly get all up in Jesus' business, but the family's matriarchy had grown deep ties with the One Above, already running a few of the church's programs, already BFF-ing the Pastores, a section of the church already partitioned off, reserved for us. My aunts, my great-aunts, and my grandmother migrated to the land of the free-to-dig-your-own-grave a few years before we did. We didn't choose our favorite Colombian restaurant (La Pequeña Colombia) or the supermarket we'd shop at (Sedano's) or the neighborhood we'd live in. As these things usually go, there was a collective understanding, a universal familial knowledge already in place, and when we arrived, we just slipped right into it. My tías showed us where to buy buñuelos, a tarjeta Orbitel to call Colombia, cheap milk, Venezuelan goodies, cheap gas. They knew about the best public schools and, of course, about the one-of-a-kind Colombian Christian church everyone attends. Like those families who all wear fluorescent pink shirts at amusement parks to identify each other—that's us. A herd of fluorescent immigrant women forever following Jesus' light. And I'm the queer kid who rips her pink shirt off and runs naked through the park.

I fight my mama daily. I don't want to hang out at the mall with the youth group, I don't give one fuck about the women's Bible-study group, I hate every single soft-rock Christian CD on the planet, I abhor the Pastora's smiley fake face every Sunday as she greets me with a *Que Dios te bendiga, mi niña!* Plus we moved from Bogotá right when my sexual compass's north fogged with a terrible yearning to kiss any girl. All the time. We'd left our lives in Bogotá and all I got was an "I <3 Jesus" T-shirt and a fan. Everything known to us replaced with 90% humidity and enough loneliness to kill a carnaval. My cousins, my sister, and every other member of the matriarchy understands the importance of receiving Jesucristo in your heart, and Mami can't figure out why I don't. Don't you want to be saved? What is wrong with you, nena?

When the alabanza ends, Mami suggests I join the youth group, which splits off from the main group for its own sermon every Sunday. The air smells of hairspray, Pine-Sol, and AC. The AC always dries out my eyes and reminds me this is Miami, a place so hot it's like walking through an endless labyrinth of warm jelly. This is Miami, I'm fifteen.

I'm not leaving, I say to Mami and stay to watch the Pastor deliver yet another stunning lecture on the importance of the nuclear family staying together despite obstacles, despite the satanic media's opinions about divorce, despite not loving each other. *Love can be built, created. For instance, mi hermano, when was the last time you bought her flowers?* Manly voices chuckle. *Marriage is a sacred bond for life. It is the basis of society, and it is under threat.*

I scan the room searching for a face of recognition, for someone here as lost as I am. I smile at a young boy, but he looks at me in judgment, pointing to the stage where I should concentrate my attention. I scan again. I scan for someone undone. Someone who shouldn't be thinking about eating pussy but, like me, can't help it. I only trust people who are visibly fucked up. Everyone is nodding, arms extended, lost in the Pastor's words. Nobody's thinking of pussy. Sólo yo. Every time the Pastor says, *Mujeres en Dios*, I'm up in the sky, not kicking it with Papi Dios as I should but rather floating in and out of her thighs.

I spend my time at church deciding how gay I am. I can't even think of the word "gay" yet, but I pass time measuring hetero vs. homo thoughts, flogging myself à la Opus Dei for being such a satanic, shameful piece of horny flesh. I want to be different, but I don't want to be a homo. Homos are hairdressers and PE teachers. Homos are unlovable, unfuckable, and opposite to God's Word. And I don't even know any homos. Once, in Catholic school, we all teased a boyish girl for being a lesbiana, asquerosa, inmunda. Gross, qué asco. We needed to keep her away so as not to be contaminated by her masculine pants, short hair, the way she kicked a soccer ball better than we did. In retrospect, I think we all wanted to bang her, but that addictive feeling of superiority in belonging to something, being part of something, took over.

At church, I don't belong to anything, and nothing belongs to me. I try reaching for my mother, my sister, anyone in my family, but they belong to the congregation, and the congregation belongs to Jesús, and apparently Jesús talks to everyone but me. I imagine Jesús watching me stare at the dancer's hair, imagine him in his brown robe all bloody from the crucifixion but still with enough energy to throw me a side-eye and shut the door to His house.

I can't even conceive of the thought of homos without a ball of needles running through my veins, smashing into my head. So, my querido reader, I've put systems in place. I have a notebook where I write checks every time I think or feel something hetero and Xs every time I think or feel something homo. The boy with nice hair? Check. Some tía's tits pointing at the bathroom mirror? An X, clearly. Sometimes I balance my gayness by staring at the church's drummer, the Pastores' son, whose skinny, pretty face reminds me of a girl I knew back home. Faint mustache, sharp cheekbones. I try imagining how his lips must feel—thick, slimy—but then I'm thinking of the girl back home undressing for ballet class.

El cuerpo siempre va a pedir placer, the Pastor yells into the microphone, but we have to work on our spirit, strengthen our soul, so we don't give in to the temptations of the body.

Amén! The crowd nods, some even jump in agreement.

God wants your entire devotion! Not pieces, but your entire life and spirit devoted to Him.

I eye my notebook, where the Xs clearly outnumber the checks, and a feeling of doom perches on my stomach. This is 2003, mi vida, and there's no rainbow flag around to cover Jesus. At least not in this place that Colombians and Venezuelans have colonized with their newly evangelical churches, waxing salons, and bakeries. None of these bitches want to destabilize or break the uniformity of their highlighted hair and tight rhinestone jeans, the godly devotion in our DNA, or that unflattering compulsory assimilation.

Mami's eyes are shut, arms extended, swaying in prayer to the Lord. *It is in God*, the Pastor finishes, *that we shall find peace and meaning.* Mami nods, and I see her drifting away.

Before Miami, Mami and I sang "Menudo" in front of the hallway mirror. She taught me how to vibrate my shoulders to the rhythm of Wilfrido Vargas by standing erect against the wall and shaking my arms until my shoulders followed the merengue beat. Patiently, she'd stand next to me, cup my shoulders in her hands, and slowly move them, waiting for me to catch up to her pace. We were a duo dinámico. Mami was a goddess radiating puro tumbao. There was nothing Mami couldn't do, no one she couldn't take on, and when I looked up at her back then, a swirling feeling of peace, a warm connection, swam in my belly. We were two and two.

Now, after joining the church, she drifts away, slowly then quickly, like an air balloon. Like she's standing on one of those moving walkways at the airport and I'm standing on the floor and she's holding her Bible so tight it leaves an imprint on her blouse and the walkway moves and Mami's shrinking by the second, by the day, by the months that pass without us noticing, and, before you know it, Mami's nowhere to be found. She's so close to God, and I'm so far away. The rest of the matriarchy joins the walkway, chitchatting, sipping on their tintos. They, too, shrink with every prayer, every song, every youth-group meeting.

On Saturdays, our family meets at my tía's for onces. The conversation always falls on some church chisme, about how Fulanita shouldn't be leading the women's group because she's divorced, or about the pastora's preference of gold ribbon over silver ribbon for the dancers, or about the angelic voice of the pastor's son who's a true hijo de Jesús.

Or, my favorite, about finding us all good Christian men and women. Amén. We no longer listen to Wilfrido, no longer salsa to Jerry. Instead, piles of CDs with pictures of doves, crosses, and happy nuclear families on them accumulate beside the stereo. If boredom has a face, it is *this* girl at the dining table as my family is about to pray for the fifth time over the arroz con pollo. And if anxiety has a name, it is me erasing the Xs in my notebook during these family meetings, imagining ways to write more checks, deleting homo desire by accepting touch, kisses, fingers that will pull me closer to God and therefore closer to the matriarchy. My motto? El que peca y reza empata.

Of course I fail. Again and again, terribly. The more I try, the more I morph into one big walking X. And everyone in the family knows and they whisper to Mami about it and the Pastores know and Mami sends me to speak with them and the Pastores pray for me, over me, and I kneel and they chant and everyone is asking Diosito to displace all the demons in me, to gentrify my heart. But nothing leaves. All my demons stay cozy inside me, reproducing like rabbits.

QUIÉREME

Agosto 7

I took a taxi from Ale's house this morning at 8 am. Woke up wanting to throw shit and cry and have a mera mera Amazonian woman slap me dry until I was numb and alive. What happened: I met Alejandra at Precita, and when I got there homegirl was flirting with this boy who she swears she doesn't have a thing for but of course she does, and their interaction was all too boring and subtle for me and their eyes tiernitos smiling at each other over shitty beer, the promise of everlasting love deep within them. Like I needed another reminder of how unfit for love I am. Like I needed this flirtatious bullshit. I kept trying to break their gentle spell so they would just admit they wanted to hump each other dry and we could move on with this horrid trip called life. I yelled at both, *WE'RE ALL HORNY, right? Aren't we all horny? Who are you horny for?* And they both laughed in a cautious, gentle laugh, and I wanted to kill them. Por Dios, homie. Ale is a cancer and this kid is probably another really soft, gentle sign that wouldn't kill a mosca and he smiles and is courteous, says please and thank you. KILLS ME. He giggles when I say I wanna kill them for being soft.

I came to Alejandra because I broke things off with Laura. My wife. The mera mera ex-queen of my heart. My wife of five fucking years and now my friend is sitting across me ignoring everything I say but speaking to this kid in soft, giggly spurs. Oh look at the music, oh this happened to me yesterday, laugh, laugh, laugh, and he's like a tender piece of lamb waiting to be eaten by Ale and returns the favor with other average and amusing stories about so and so and laugh laugh laugh. This goes on for minutes and minutes and years and it doesn't seem to stop.

GO FUCK SOMEWHERE AND LEAVE ME ALONE.

I don't know what I was thinking. Maybe that I'd stop feeling like such a piece of shit if I went to see Ale. So I get there high and have my flask filled with aguardiente and I want my lesbro friend to lez out with me and talk ass and pussy and how much we love Latinas and shit but no, esos ojitos de ella perdidos and this kids' eyes are also shining and we're sitting in this apartment in The Mission listening to tambores, listening to people sing beautifully about gentrification, violence, listening to my heart trying to leave me, trying to escape.

I took a taxi at 8 am because when I woke up I thought I was gonna break some shit if I didn't. The driver played classical music and offered gum and water. *Strawberry please*, I say. My mouth tastes like dead mouse. The city is gray over gray in the morning and a terrifying feeling of peace bathes me for a second—this always happens. I like the city in the early dawn, I love the crisp morning smell of cold. The violence of a new blue day arriving like it's not a big deal. I hated it in Miami, but here it's like it speaks to the way my bones feel: misty, falling apart, but full of possibility. I should only be awake from 4 am–2 pm, after that living becomes unbearable: There's the yuppies lining up for brunch, their bermudas and flip-flops, their Aryan techie faces smiling from their perfected glasses, perfected lives, eating $200 pizza because they can, because they're happy, because, "Money doesn't buy happiness," said no one ever unless you're poor.

But you know what I really want to do? Call Lorrie Moore and ask to be her baby sitter. Her right-hand mama. Favorite fairy-queen. My God, that's exactly what I want. Leave this place, drive into that small town where she waits for me outside of her house, squinting as the taxi approaches, hand over eyes, cigarette on lips, a summer threadbare dark yellow dress that she reminds me is a hand-me-down from her dead mother who never loved her. Her sad look a relief. I'm in her living room, dinning room, smoking cigarettes (I would do ANYTHING FOR LORRIE), she says things like, *I hate your haircut, Juliana, get another one.* We watch old Hollywood movies with subtitles but never in our PJs, always perfectly dressed up, in full fucking drag. It takes us two hours to get ready every night. Lorrie demands I wear my black, shiny wig and the fake fur coat. It's part of our agreement. She wears dark-red lipstick and long, black gloves. I French-braid her hair before bed. My nails are always painted yellow. That's how she wants it. She lives in this small town, in a two-bedroom house with her child. She writes all day and I watch her in awe because, of course, my hero but, also, she murmurs every sentence and walks in circles with a pink Post-it on hand until the moment comes to her and then you can see the right words making their way up from her gut to her brain and then the murmuring mouth. She scribbles on the Post-it with an irrefutable sense of success that's only visible in her breathing. She plays it cool, but I know she's got it because her eyes get a certain luminosity and she blinks incessantly.

Stop looking at me for Christ sakes, she says.

We're drunk all day because it's summer and she doesn't teach. We try taking walks together around the lake, but we can't stand each other. We fight over who should be walking on the left side. I'm totally obsessed with her in a non-sexual way, and she becomes the first woman I can love with no sexual intimacy. She doesn't want me to do anything for her, only make her breakfast and read the obituaries out loud on Sundays. *You have an extraordinary voice*, she says, *like a newscaster or those guys narrating soccer matches*. On Sundays, too, we go to church together. Neither of us believes in Jesus but we pretend we're a family. This time I wear a tie, hair slick back with gel. I carry the baby. We pray. We know all the prayers. We sing. Some people invite us to their houses for dinner, we decline. We're tired. Nobody knows I'm female, nobody knows Lorrie is not gay. She wears all black, always, but her house is full of flowers and green plants, some of which have long been dead. One day at the end of summer while we're both reading in opposite sides of her living room, she gently removes her glasses and says: *Why are you still here?*

Agosto 9

Laura left today, and I couldn't sleep last night trying to hug her, reaching for her tits. I kept waking up totally lost, I had no idea who was with me in bed. I bit her back but it was when I grabbed her tits that I knew it was her. At some point I pulled her hair, and she told me to stop.

Is someone fucking you that hard? she's been asking me.

The day before yesterday (the night, really), we drank aguardiente, listened to motherfucking vallenatos (cause that's how we get down) and talked about ourselves, each other, this studio, that picture, that wavy scar she has on her back from the first date she had with this girl and came back all bruised and scratched, and I threw shit. We talked and cried. Like good lesbians, a lot of staring. A lot of this relationship changed my life. A lot of why is this happening. Because, why, really. But also: no other way. No other way.

There are places inside you where I haven't been, she said.

I know, I said. *But you've travelled so much deeper than anyone I've known.*

We drank so much. Shot after shot after shot of aguardiente. At some point I stood up and started dancing salsa by myself. Amores como el nuestro quedan ya muy pocos—*Jerry you are forever breaking my heart*—she laughed, smiled, tilted her head in an I-know-you kinda way. I stared at those brown, skinny motherfucking gorgeous arms of hers, how they move gracefully, sometimes clumsy, as they grab my face and kiss me, as her tears blend with mine. I really wanted to fuck, but we couldn't. There was no way we were fucking like that. There's a part of myself, most of myself, that's unmoved. In total state of shock. Like when I sat next to her in that blue couch, in that house which is ours but not really because rent, but ours because our hearts and love and that new kitchen stuff we bought. And I remember in my drunkness staring at the Ikea bookshelf that Adela help us hook to the wall. *Permanently*, she said, *the way we tried hooking our relationship*, and I thought how much of a pain in the ass it was going to be to unhook it, how the wall was going to crumble, how there was probably some permanent damage left on that wall and there was nothing we could do.

There's a picture of us in that bookshelf smiling like dumb fucks on our first trip up north to Mendocino. Laura's hair is long and red, mine is long and curly and we're smiling on a mountain, the ocean infinite behind us. I remember the guy we asked to take the picture said, *Welcome to America,* and we both burst out laughing. You dumb gringo bitch.

Look at us, Laura said pointing at the picture.

Agosto 10

This morning we took the train together—*FOR THE LAST TIME*, we both said. She's so excited about the breakup. Like it's her first day at a new school.

You're so excited cause this is your first breakup and it's not even that bad, I said.

What you mean?

I mean, I'm here kissing you and saying goodbye. You wanna see bad breakups? I've had bad breakups. I've had bitches throwing shit on me on the street. I've travelled to other countries and yelled at a window. This is so civil.

The night of the aguardiente, I passed out before throwing up but she threw up before passing out. She hugged the toilet, she told me later, and wasn't sure how she stumbled to bed. The next morning: hangover, kisses, her period. I made her breakfast, tea, warm bag for her belly. *I fucking love you, girl,* I wanna say all the time like that's gonna bring her back to me. Bring me back my wife that I loved, that went to Dolores Park with me and got drunk and read poems and beat me up and fucked me so good and cut my hair and watched nature documentaries and let me lick her face in the morning and her smell and the diamond tattoo. She's moving to Berkeley today, and I'm alive. We sang Shakira last night while cooking. It seems like all is piling up. Like time ain't moving forward but circular. Like I'm repeating myself because I am. Here we are breaking up. Here we are unhooking that shelf. Here we are. But then kissing, then crying, then breaking up again, then fucking but crying and staring at old pictures. Bring her back to me.

Agosto 11

Yesterday, I went to the beach. When I got home there was no fog: surprise! So I put on my faggy running shoes and went for it. All the way to the beach, running for my fucking life until my lugs exploded in my face and I was drenched in something pure. I bought an acaí bowl and walked to the ocean. Sat there thinking about nothing, or, maybe, about taking a Snapchat of this moment which I fucking did. "LOOK AT HOW BEAUTIFUL MY LIFE IS EVEN THOUGH IM MISERABLE." That should have been the caption. "LOOK AT ME, GODDAMN IT. MY LIFE IS FALLING APART BUT HEY I'M USING THIS HAPPY FILTER. IM SO HAPPY." The sun was totally killing it. Queen-like, fierce as fuck. Glimmering in the ocean for days, for miles on end and the mountains around, the small houses on Ocean Beach leaning against each other like a pack of pale sardines. It's almost like being somewhere else.

Agosto 17

My mom this morning: *Tus tías están muy preocupadas.*
Ah, si? I say. *Why?*
Because, mami continues, *te ves terrible and sad in all your pictures.*

They don't understand why. They wanna know.

Gracias, mom. Gracias.

We drove down to Santa Cruz in Virgie's old-ass champagne-colored car and met Jerry Lee for his birthday at the boardwalk. Driving down in that car feels like a movie, old school as fuck, driving slow in the right lane with nothing to freaking lose. Like that movie, *Buffalo 66*, but instead of two white people it's Virgie and I pretending we're not heartbroken. Or escaping the heartbreak, leaving it contained in San Francisco, sending it to the mountains, the ocean that opens up infinitely blue and terrifying. Christina Ricci in the back softly nodding to everything we say, singing Stevie Nicks and weirdly photobombing our selfies. Christina lays on the hotel bed with me and when I put my head on her belly she tells me I have thin hair and scars on my skull. Christina never kisses me.

We cruised the boardwalk, up and down, staring at nipples and dicks and contemplating how beautiful people look in the dark. We went on all the rides: the Giant Dipper, Double Shot, haunted house. I had some shitty coffee that, again, gave me the shitz. Even though it's California, the boardwalk is like an American Movie in *real life*. What I imagined when I lived in Colombia: fried Twinkies, fried Oreos, corndogs, hot dogs, fried artichoke. Extra-large everything. All in one place. The air was crisp and warm. We ate poke bowls and organic ice cream, we watched the Food Network and tallied how many people we'd fucked. We walked barefooted on the beach, rocks sticking to our soles.

Agosto 20

1. My in-laws sent me messages via WhatsApp. Laura's parents, both of them. First, her mom's messages, two hours later her dad's. I imagine María (Mom) telling Ricardo (Dad) to please mi amor, send her a message, we're all in this. I imagine her rallying up the family around this—Colombian people mi amor, the entire family is expected to be involved in everyone's matters. It is a matter of public opinion. A town hall. I get anxious as fuck. I stare at the phone without totally reading the message or else she'll know (thank you, WhatsApp). I don't respond. I want the world to be obtuse, to recline so I stop feeling like such a dumbass.

2. I only cried once today. Went for a run to the beach, then açaí bowl, then walk back. BE INTENTIONAL MOTHERFUCKER. I try.

But then I opened the door to my house and it just comes POURING out of my eyes like the rain in Bogotá. One second sunshine the next is an hijueputa aguacero. Like cum in your mouth and there's nothing you can do to stop it. I squirted through my eyes into this studio until my books were swimming.

3. Cooked tacos with Ale today. Went for a walk afterwards to Mitchell's cause homegirl desperately wanted some ice cream. As we walked down Bryant street, I saw two old Asian people inside a building smoking and coughing. *This is all they do*, Ale says.

What you mean?

This is all they do. They sit behind that fence and smoke and cough all day.

Really? I say. I imagine my lungs opening up to the smoke, imagine taking all of it in. Imagine a life where all I did was hustle for cigarettes and stare at a street filled with dog shit and white hipsters.

Agosto 21

I'm reading Barthes' *A Lover's Discourse,* of which I understand one-fourth, but I'm trying so hard on the train going home. It's 9 pm. The other day, I saw pigeon wings on the street. Bloody wings perfectly arranged against the gray pavement. I thought it was some trash bag on the street, but as I moved closer I saw the bird with no body. There was something so tender about it. I wanted it to pick it up and yell, *GOD WHY ARE YOU SENDING ME METAPHORS! AT LEAST IF YOU'RE SENDING METAPHORS MAKE ME WORK HARDER TO FIGURE THEM OUT.* A bird with no wings? Please. Disembodied wings? Mi reina, por favor. I stood staring down at the wings, the grey, white and black feathers hardened already, the blood so red almost fake, almost too Tarantino for me. I yell at God every time I stumble upon some clear metaphor for my life: dreams of me yelling at my father. Dead shit on the ground. An old fashionable granny screaming on the bus. ALL TOO CLEAR. I like *working* for meaning. I like figuring shit out. I'm a Gemini, Diosito, in case you forgot. I could tell the wings were already stiff. At first I thought it was a black trash bag, but as I got closer the form mutated into feathers, into greys and whites into blood and cartilage and whatever else makes up birds. Bird body. Some people walked pass me, watched me, then stared at the wings and when they realized it wasn't some spectacle continued walking disappointed by my curiosity.

On the train, I'm reading, staring at my half reflection, at the vague outline of my face: two black holes, lines mapping my mouth—I'm getting old. There's also a black cap, a black scarf. There are places on my face that I don't recognize so I don't stare for too long.

A woman asks, *Where are we?*

I tell her we're almost at 19th Ave.

Really? she says.

Ajá, I respond.

Only 19th?

I know girl, I wanna say. *I also wish I was passed this moment already, already somewhere else beyond this point, I've also been waiting for 19th to pass quickly, but it seems stuck.*

Agosto 23

1. Laura walked naked around the garden this morning, I watched her body stretch, her arms raised to the white sky, her ribs like train tracks on her back. That beautiful, bouncy ass. That meaty ass. Those legs that welcomed me. Not this time. I laid on a towel waiting to dry, feeling my heart beating on my butt, always waiting for something to happen. Long, bright trees reaching for her body, enclosing us both. She's beautiful and awake and independent and far away and not with me. But we're here. There are two black cats meowing between us, one licks her hip bone. She watches. She says, *They never do this when I'm here alone.* We go back to the hot tub. I try holding her hand, but it's awkward in the water and, anyway, what are we trying to do. What are we trying to prove. We're done. What am I doing. Watching her take the world in. Watching how the world works on her body and that spirit of hers drifting above me or below but never in the same place as mine.

Laura is staying in this room in Berkeley and there's a "public" bathtub in the house next door. It's one of those bathtubs for hippies, Buddhists, and all those who love the woo, especially women. So we wake up at 6 am and walk the walk to the tub and undress and shower, and I'm following her because I know nothing of this ritual. We're all naked. We're all too alive right now. It's 6 am in Berkeley and my wife who's not my wife showers in the tiny shower next to the tub, I pass the towel, she dries in her own way, she dries arms first, legs last. Jet black bush curling up and I wanna dive into her. Laura has the most beautiful pussy I've ever seen. She knows this. I tell her all the time. I tell her she should exhibit that pussy cause it's SO PRETTY. Like God really took her time. God was all like, bring me some coffee for this one, bring me my best stencil.

2. I cried so much at the Elbo Room last night I thought they were gonna kick me out. For crying. For messing their shitty furniture with my female tears. We sat on the booths in the back and Laura ordered us gin and tonic. My napkin was all wet, my eyes were all wet, my pussy was DRY. We can't be together, and I know that. What am I expecting? I don't know. I texted her earlier in the day wanting to see her. (*MOM: WHY DID YOU GIVE ME SUCH HORRIBLE BOUNDARIES, AH?*) I texted her because even though we have therapy (yes, queen) on Wednesday, there are things I can't say in front of other people. Even with our therapist.

That's one of Laura's complaints: *I've realized I don't really know you, know you*, she said.

What you mean?

I've been surprised many times in therapy because there are things and places I don't know of you. That sucks. I thought everything was on the table, she says all saddened.

I said, *HOW MANY TIMES DO YOU THINK I'VE CRIED IN PUBLIC FOR A GIRL? None.*

She's the first one. It's true.

Am I supposed to feel special? she says. *Am I supposed to hang to the fact that this is the first time you're doing this?*

I couldn't drink the gin and tonic. I told her I missed cuddling her, smelling that neck, burying my face into her hair.

I don't want to be with you but I miss you, I said.

You contradict yourself all the time, she responds.

3. I bought a ticket to see my mom. Go to the ocean. Watch old white people burn under the sun. Watch something burn, something else that's not me.

Agosto 24

Took off wedding ring today. Kept touching the dent in my finger all day.

Septiembre 6

This is how you get over a broken heart:

You buy a ticket to Miami with the money you'd been saving with your ex-boo. You swim and run every day. You eat home-cooked meals and meditate. You run errands with your mama, try on quinceañera dresses while your mother snaps pictures and then you cry a little in the bathroom because you DID WEAR A FUCKING BIG WEDDING DRESS AND NOW ALL IS RUINED. But it's not. You swim and run the next day. You journal your way through every single anxiety: I will never find anyone else. Nobody will ever love me again. I can't live alone. I can't stay in this relationship, etc. You eat arepas and ajiaco while braiding your mama's hair and doing your nails. You have to travel to a warm place where there's water. You take sad selfies that you don't post on Instagram. You're the biggest faggot in all Florida wearing heels and lipstick up and down the street while homeboys wash their cars and look at you in disgust. BUT YOU'RE A MOTHERFUCKING QUEEN. You yell at yourself in the bathroom mirror: *YOU'RE A FUCKING REINA MI AMOR* and then you cry and then you meditate and then you call on that inner goddess and she sends Toni Morrison and she sends *Beloved* and she sends Roland Barthes and Sylvia Plath and a cute straight girl at the supermarket flirts with you. You watch documentaries of Juan Gabriel with your mother, you sing Juan Gabriel with your mother. You belong to something grand, something bigger than yourself, something bigger than this pain. You swim and run again. You swim underwater holding your breath for as long as you can until you feel your soul leaving you, until you turn to the sky which gives you nothing but that heartbeat and your lungs full of life. You write lists. You're down to only checking her Instagram once a day and you never check her Facebook. You go to the ocean and try not to drown. You take your BFF's advice about being alone, about diving into the unknown, about being present with your pain. You have no idea how to do any of this but you try. You fail and cry again. You mess up and cry again. You wanna go back to her warmth but you remember you can't act on fear. You eat cold pressed juices and buy cheap shit at Walmart—you sing reggaetón in the car with your mother. You remember things from your childhood.

Octubre 20

Laura and I had dinner last night. She bought a new grey hat that makes her look like such an artsy beautiful thing. But there was something strange yesterday. I brought her this book at Modern Times because they're closing and everything is 20% off and it's devastating but that's not where I'm going with this. The book is of this T-Rex with small hands who can't do anything human. In the story, T-Rex fails at the most random and basic things in life. I limped my way to the restaurant cause my foot is fucked up from running. Laura tells me all about the rooms she's been seeing, where she's gonna move, the work. There are times when I just want to kiss her, but yesterday was not one of those. I kept trying to have her say something beautiful and deep but it didn't happen. I kept telling myself, I'll give her the present at the right time. The right time seemed to never materialize. I was so disappointed—I will see Andrea today, in a bit, and she'll say something about her ex that reminds me of myself (and why do Geminis have such a big fucking ego?) how she always had to thank her every bit of the way as they were getting divorced. And it made me think of that moment this night with Laura as I wait for the right moment because I want a certain kind of energy, certain kind of feeling from her that I'm not getting.

When I finally give her the book, her eyes water. She puts it in her purse real quick. Like she doesn't want that feeling to linger for too long, but all I want is for the feeling to linger for long. For her to want me. She looks down and says *Ay, Juliana. Ay, Juliana.* She doesn't want to investigate that feeling. But I bring it back. I tell her to look through the book. She does. We laugh together at the clumsiness. She mimics the dinosaur putting her hands out like they're dead, dropping from her chest. This always made me love her and super uncomfortable. Her inner child so visible to the public eye, mine definitely hidden deep inside. Her level of ease with displaying this child in public sometimes made me uncomfortable—I think about this often. How my mother always wanted a perfected public image. How nothing was every discussed on the streets or in front of people but always at home. How I self-policed myself (and have been doing this forever) to always seem put together, strong, self-reliant. The problem with this is my intimate relationships expect this, I go into a relationship with this tough carcass that's supposed to save me. Whenever people disclose stuff from their very personal lives I'm in awe—completely flabbergasted at the lack of self-containment and vergüenza.

Noviembre 18

I'm a blob of coffee and nails. A red balloon. If you pop me nails will fly everywhere; one may even kill you. I'm a walking time bomb. Mornings of crying, masturbating thinking of that girl, that internet crush, that fake blow job of a fake dick that feels so good as I grab your hair and pull you. Then cry. I don't know what day it is. I count the days backwards trying to remember. I'm doing the minimum to keep this shit afloat: I do the emails, I take a shower. I buy cereal and eat it. Pretend I'm part of the world by posting stupid shit on the internetz. I plan things for the day that don't happen. I imagine myself reading, writing, clear-headed—someone else. I wish I had the strength to not be an idiot. I wish I had the strength to do what these white people seem so good at: denial and brunch parties. Today is Friday. Thursday was yesterday and the day before was also Thursday and Tuesday didn't happen. There was no Tuesday. That day I cried until I couldn't see anymore and then the joke was on me when I found a sty on my eye and now I can't really see shit. My body reacting to all this horrific shit. On Facebook, someone boasts lovingly about a new anti-depressant. I search for it. I want something to clean my fucking insides. I feel like a walking joke and I don't understand how people are interacting and continuing. It's not only about Trump. But I'm a stable person, a sane person. Lo que diga el dedito mamita. Messy, Queen. I got my period, uterus throbbing reminding me of the punishment for not being pregnant. I wish I could like someone. At least. I wanna host a brunch inspired by white people's brunches where all we do is sit around denying shit happens while licking off mayonnaise from our fingers.

Noviembre 29

Bitch, is it a new day or what? Am I feeling better or what? The sun is peaking over my window, saying hello mami you knew I wouldn't leave you alone. But you was a stupid bitch for a second there, you needed to. Writing from my new house. I'm trying out this new thing in which I write in the mornings, first thing. I can't keep postponing it cause I'll never get to it. Fucking cold is what it is but im happy. Am I? Is this happiness? What is it? I may even go outside for coffee after my meeting today. I have a whole hour to write. I got no one to bother me. No one to take care of. Already listened to Rachel Maddow lecture me on the apocalyptic comings of the orange fart ball's cabinet picks. This new feeling of being alone. Of choosing to be alone. Not lonely. Just really seeing the contours of my body, where it is ends and how it doesn't blend with anyone's. Laura and I mesh into one big Mami Monster. It was cute. It was. How I sometimes saw her as my extension, how I knew what she needed before she did (like Amazon!) but it's been one-and-a-half days (NOT EVEN) of total detachment. Of this is me. I end here in this chopped-off nail and toe and here are my ribs, each one on their own.

We moved out of the apartment this past weekend. A bunch of dykes, Miah, and Armando helped me out. Laura was there, too. She shaved her head. Did I write that already? She did. It looks good on her. Little punk kid. I love playing with her head now. We've been so tender and loving with each other. I held her as much as I could trying hard to hold on to the last remnants of this and when we parted she said I could stay with her and I wanted to, but then what? I had to start somewhere. It seems like the most banal and easy thing to do: not sleep with her that night. Be alone. But it took everything I had to say, *No, thank you.* I'm staying home now. In this little room with the window and the sun peaking in, like company. We've been through the peak, I felt it. The moment we moved. And stacking boxes in pick-up trucks with all my dyke friends carrying pieces of our (my) lives, dismembering what was left of this Mami Monster. I felt the peak of this shit in my lungs a few days before. The night of Thanksgiving at tía cathy's house. Adela made Cuban-style Thanksgiving, so instead of turkey she cooked a pierna de pernil. Cooked chicken for *this* faggot. Most of my queer family was there. Adela the big queer mama as the head of the household. A bunch of old Cuban locas, dykes, and fags showed up. Me, the only one below 50 years old. Ornella was there. We smoked and drank champagne. Ornella is like 60, and I like her. I love her accent, and she has this clear blue dictatorial eyes. Not celestial, but piercing and kinda fascist. She's Italian, that's why. Straight but dresses like a dyke. When she got there she said, *Oh, Adela said there were already a bunch of lesbians here but it's only you*. She wears black manly shoes and has wavy dark brown hair below her shoulders. She's the kinda bitch who would slap you while smoking a cigarette and then shoot you and continue cooking, bitching about how you bothered her. Don't bother her, she'll shoot you.

Thanksgiving night. My lungs dying. Taking selfies with my mama and her colitas. She wears two ponytails cause she can't blow dry that hair. Shingles. Mama got shingles in Miami and now she can't move her arm.

I couldn't breathe this weekend. Now I drink licorice tea and make potions for my body. My lungs will slowly recover. Dear computer. Dear me. Dear sun at my window.

ACKNOWLEDGEMENTS

Many thanks to the editors of the following sites on which some of these pieces appeared, sometimes in slightly different versions: "The Boy Who Never Cried For Me," *Midnight Breakfast* (Issue 14); "The Fake People I've Loved" *Weird Sister* (January 2015).

JULIANA DELGADO LOPERA is an award-winning Colombian writer based in San Francisco. The recipient of the 2014 Jackson Literary award, she's the author of *¡Cuéntamelo!*, an illustrated bilingual collection of oral histories by LGBT Latin@ immigrants. Her work has been nominated for a Pushcart Prize and published in various publications. She's the executive director of RADAR Productions.